A GIFT FOR ~

Knowing Beautiful

A new bedtime story for women

with a Guided Journal

celebrating your beautiful Spirit Meredith! Love, Amy

Amy Tirion

Buoyancy Books
San Francisco, California

Buoyancy Books
1883 17th Avenue, San Francisco, California 94122
knowingbeautiful.com

Cover, Book Design, and Illustrations: Robyn Lomauro Grenning

printed on wood-free paper in china

ISBN # 978-1-4675-6380-2
10 9 8 7 6 5 4 3 2 1

AN INVITATION

You have an abundant source of beauty that is deeper than your skin and fuller than your shape. It is a beauty that grows within as you learn to see yourself, in all that you do, in all that you are, in all you touch with your heart, in all that you impact with your energy and talents, and in all that you lift up with your grace.

Often your own story gets in the way of living in your place of beauty. You have worked years to write the story of how you see yourself. It has chapters written by others, by society, and by your own inner critic. This story is waiting to be rewritten.

Knowing Beautiful is a gentle invitation to write your own story, through a lens of compassion, pride, clarity, and love for the full beauty of you. May this story help you to see a more beautiful blossoming reflection of yourself. May the guided journal inspire you to deepen your connection with the truest, most beautiful part of you.

LOOK DEEPLY.
YOU'LL FIND HER.

You are a fabulously Capable and Calm woman.

You appear younger than your years

because you can't be bothered with the idea
that you don't do Enough.

INSTEAD YOU MOVE THROUGH EACH DAY WITH EASE,

swaying between
a tightly orchestrated list of priorities
and a loosely planned allowance for Inspiration.

You allow yourself the time to Stop, to Dream, and to Feel.

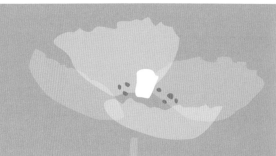

YOU HOLD YOURSELF GENTLY

in a place of knowing that you are perfectly, wonderfully just right.

You are sought after for your
Energy and Wisdom.

YOUR ENERGY YOU SHARE CAREFULLY,

always having enough sips
for yourself before bed.

YOUR WISDOM YOU SHARE OPENLY,

but only after asking a few clarifying questions
to help others find their own answers.

YOU ARE COMFORTABLE WITH RISK,

knowing that it makes you stronger

AND A FRIEND OF SLOW,
Knowing that it keeps you soft.

YOU ALWAYS SLEEP WELL, UNDER A BLANKET OF TRUST.

Worry is not in your vocabulary. You prefer the word care. You fall asleep knowing you care about your relationships, your children, your career, your financial situation, your future, and you care about the world.

In the morning you wrap your arms around
what you care about with fresh
Capacity, Faith, Courage, and Calm.

YOUR BEAUTY GROWS WITH EACH PASSING YEAR

as you discover what makes you feel most alive

and carve out the time
        to nurture that part
of yourself.

OTHERS CAN FEEL YOUR ENERGY.

Your Vitality draws others to you.

Being in your company
Inspires others to work a little more
on their own fulfillment.

Whether it is Growing your career,
growing your spirit, growing your intellect,
growing your children, or growing your garden...
maybe it is feeling strong in your body, helping others,
or creating something new...

WHAT MAKES YOU FEEL MOST ALIVE CHANGES OVER TIME AND HAS MANY LAYERS. You always hold that part of yourself sacred, share it openly, and encourage others to Blossom.

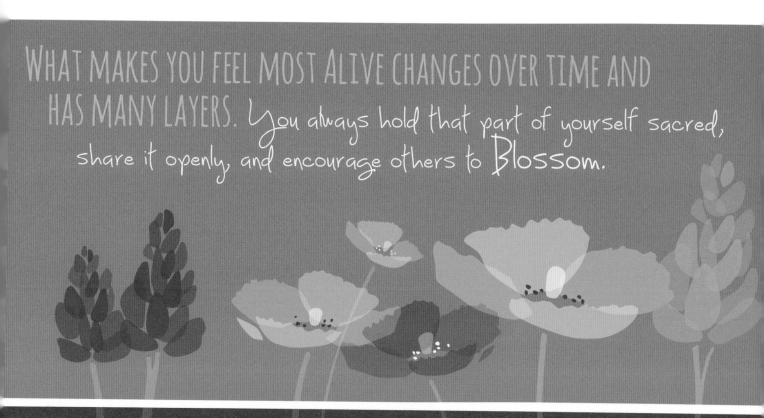

Joy flows through you.

You live in your senses and breathe gratitude.

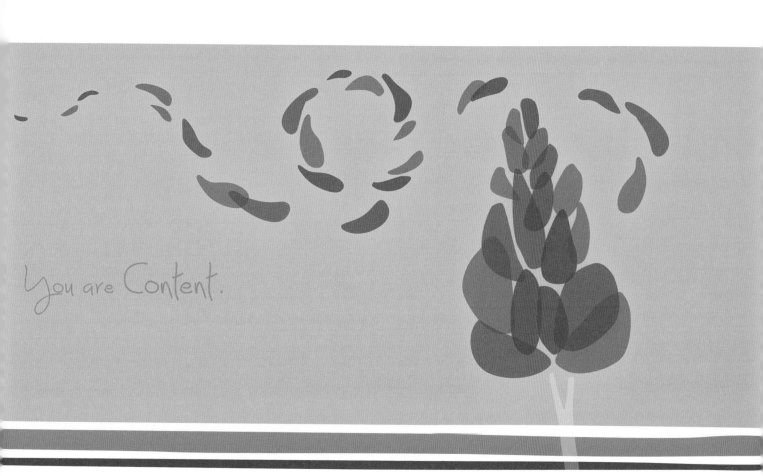

You are Content.

YOUR HEART LIVES OUT LOUD.

You are Vulnerable.

It takes Courage, but you find
Strength in your Authenticity.

You know Beautiful.

It is Deeply You.

28

GUIDED JOURNAL

The following pages invite you to go inward, exploring and expanding your sense of Self.
Take a page at a time, in any order. You can just think about your answers, write them or draw them, either in the book or elsewhere. As time goes on, you may add to your observations. You may also take this journey with others - a friend, a book group, or a women's circle.

Deepening your connection with yourself will reveal a new reflection: you are rich in beauty. Your beauty rests in your quiet center of authenticity, in your gentle compassion for yourself, how you touch the world around you, and most importantly, in the loving relationship you create with yourself.

It is time to write your own story . . .

I AM CAPABLE AND CALM.

Describe what being capable feels like · · ·

I HAVE SELF-COMPASSION.

I can be more gentle with myself by . . .

I DO ENOUGH.

I don't always need to do as much as I can every day. Instead I want to allow time for . . .

32

I AM FILLED WITH EASE.

At the end of the day, what is most important . . .

I AM A DREAMER.

A dream or desire that I want to keep alive . . .

I AM WHOLE.

The parts of me where I want to shift self-criticism to self-compassion . . .

I AM WISE. The wisdom I hold that I most trust . . .

I care for myself by . . .

I AM NOURISHED.

I AM COURAGEOUS.   Risks I have taken that have made me stronger . . .

A risk I would like to take . . .

Slowing down will help me . . .   I AM RELAXED.

I TRUST.

The areas of my life where I want to shift from worrying to trust · · ·

I HAVE VITALITY.

I feel most alive when . . .

I AM UNFOLDING.

I am personally growing . . .

42

I LOVE FREELY.

My heart lives out loud when I . . .

I AM STRONG.

Times when I have stepped into my strength . . .

I feel confident being completely me when . . .

I AM AUTHENTIC.

I feel vulnerable being completely me when . . .

I AM FULFILLED.

I feel content when . . .

I feel my beauty touches the world when I . . .

I AM DEEPLY BEAUTIFUL.

. . . go ahead, allow yourself to see.

Amy Tirion

Amy Tirion's passion is to inspire women to connect with their most joyful, wise, and beautiful selves. She is a speaker, change management consultant, writer, restorative yoga trainer, and dancer. She launched Delight for the Soul, which offers workshops and retreats for women. Amy was profiled in Elizabeth Arden's documentary series on inner beauty, entitled *Her Story*. She resides in San Francisco, where she shares her love for the arts, creativity, and essence-filled living with her husband and their two daughters.

To learn more about Amy's offerings, follow her blog, or to subscribe to her newsletter, visit amytirion.com.